SCORE!

Sarah Wardle was born and lives in London. She lectures on the BA and MA writing programmes at Middlesex University, reviews poetry for the *Observer*, and is poet-in-residence at Tottenham Hotspur Football Club. She won the Geoffrey Dearmer Prize in 1999, and her first book *Fields Away* (Bloodaxe Books, 2003), was shortlisted for the Forward Prize for Best First Collection. *Score!* (Bloodaxe Books, 2005) is her second book of poems.

SARAH WARDLE

SCORE!

Sarah Wardle

BLOODAXE BOOKS

ISBN: 1 85224 706 1

First published 2005 by
Bloodaxe Books Ltd,
Highgreen,
Tarset,
Northumberland NE48 1RP.

www.bloodaxebooks.com
For further information about Bloodaxe titles
please visit our website or write to
the above address for a catalogue.

Bloodaxe Books Ltd acknowledges
the financial assistance of
Arts Council England, North East.

Cover printing by J. Thomson Colour Printers Ltd, Glasgow.

Printed in Great Britain by
Bell & Bain Limited, Glasgow, Scotland.

To Tottenham Hotspur F.C.

ACKNOWLEDGEMENTS

Acknowledgements are due to the editors of the following publications where some of these poems first appeared: *Evening Standard, Guardian, Independent, The Interpreter's House, The Liberal, London Magazine, Orbis, Oxford Magazine* and *Soundings.*

I'm especially grateful to Donna Cullen, Fran Jones and Tottenham Hotspur Football Club for giving me the opportunity to write poems for them, to be inspired by the beautiful game at White Hart Lane, and to David Lyall and Anna Rimington for letting me help in the Spurs Study Support Centre.

I'm grateful to the programme producers for whom some of these poems were broadcast, including for: Sky Sports News, BBC World Service, BBC London Radio, BBC London TV, BBC Breakfast TV, BBC Northern Ireland, BBC Radio 5, BBC Radio 4 Woman's Hour, BBC The World/Boston, SBS Australia, ABC Australia, Oneword Radio, Capital Radio and Swedish Radio.

Some poems have appeared on the Spurs website, www.spurs.co.uk, and on www.bbc.co.uk and www.ideasfactory.com.

'Premonition' won a prize in the 2004 Keats-Shelley Poetry Competition.

CONTENTS

9   St George's Eve

In Memoriam Bill Nicholson

11   *In Memoriam* Bill Nicholson
12   In the Bill Nicholson Suite
13   Injury Room
14   Defoe
15   Keane
16   *Audere Est Facere*
17   Tottenham Hotspur 1, Blackburn Rovers 0
18   Captains
19   Late News
20   Goal
21   *In Memoriam* Sidney Wells
22   Against Metaphor
24   Kabul
25   By Hart
26   At White Hart Lane

X Poems

27   Easter X
32   To an Ex-OUCA President
34   Ex-Prospective
36   X: A Poetry Political Broadcast

Sheet Music

46   Independence Day Dawn
47   Footprints
48   Hackney Downs
49   After London
50   Sheet Music
51   Baggage
52   English Civil War
53   Premonition
54   Breakthrough
55   *Noli Me Tangere*
56   Sarah Malcolm in Prison
57   Hymn to Enlightenment
58   Balance Sheet

59 Emily's Voice
60 Indian Summer
61 Constance Ethelfleda
62 Frederick Maclean Wardle
63 Wards
64 Pacific Storm
65 Sea Views
66 Covenant
67 Finding Space for Time
68 Schrödinger's Cat
69 The Female Gaze
70 Elegy
71 Betterton Street
72 Maybe It's Because
74 New Year with Nelson
75 Under the Wave
76 Good Friday
77 May Sunday
78 On Byron Ward
79 Looking Back
80 Messenger

St George's Eve

On St George's Eve head back to the England you know,
down lanes you remember overhung with snow,
fenced grounds at the entrance to the village,
a Victorian school, the old shop, the Cat Inn. Go in,
order coffee among faces to which you half wish
you belonged, as one says 'Next time, don't leave it so long.'
Unfurl mapped memory, the smell of air that's different here,
the only place April is real. Stand by the open forge
and half see in the light of last orders
the blacksmith's scene, a nativity of time already passed.
Then climb the twisting hill to the village church.
Enter its garden of graves through the gate,
up trodden steps to stones, covered with moss.
Cry for all that was already lost.
Reach instinctively for the yew tree.
Tear at its bread to suck its smoky taste, like tea.
Walk on for miles, using your own feet now.
At the approach of engines climb the verge, glare asides.
At Gilbert's Cross turn left. Approach, then pass
the house you know every inch by heart.
Stand by a field gate to cry to full moon.
Then on past Homer's cottage, remembered autumns,
knowing this time you're going the distance.
Turn left up Hollies Lane. Retrace each ride
beneath the sky you know, cradled in contours
of familiar boundaries, priestly trees, each where it should be,
large in looming welcome. Listen like a horse,
like a dog whose bones are buried fields away,
aware for any danger, filtering, like radar, the stir of leaves,
hoots of owls, nightwatch chatter of a stream, a lamb's call,
a pheasant's startle. Walk on past intermittent farms,
sailing on the village outskirts, giant as churches.
Know at No Man's Green you'll bridge the hill.
Mount the gate for the Sheep Walk and follow the line
of old oak trees to crest the landscape you fled towards
in dreams. Let the ground gift you a stick to carry
like a staff, a wooden foot, treading the ridge like a tightrope.
Feel midnight gallop through your hair, loose as clouds
scudding across the night sun. Drink the rim

of this place, where three counties meet, like your blood.
At the other side, find only a car with sleeping lovers,
held in the muffled beat of CD sound. Circle round,
and at the crossroads choose Heron's Gate Lane,
fording forest with the road to find
you haven't lost your way and the only
silhouette of threat was April holly.

In Memoriam Bill Nicholson

You still attend each match at White Hart Lane.
As the ground empties we remember Bill.
You haven't left us. In the lit-up rain
there's music playing as your credits roll

through men's minds. Director and producer
of the Glory Years, you won the Double,
served in the army and for Tottenham Hotspur,
and scored for England against Portugal.

In the minute's silence you might have heard
a shilling, or penny drop. To a man
the stands knighted you, raised you up a Lord,
Leagues ahead on another field and plain.

But you're not gone. In these grass seeds and roots
you push on through and though flags fly half-mast,
you're the father in the sky Keane salutes
now as he scores, Spurs new blood and their past.

In the Bill Nicholson Suite

This football is a found poem.
On it Danny Blanchflower signed
the names of his winning team,
when Tottenham Hotspur completed
the Double in '61. Here are the scorers,
Smith and Dyson, and the score:
Spurs 2, Leicester City 0. And there
Bill Nicholson autographed the back
on leather the colour of faded parchment.

This football is a testament of victory,
an historical document, witness
to an age of meritocracy.
These are not the names
of hereditary kings, but of men
who succeeded and deserved to win.

This football sits in a glass case,
as if it's been kicked
straight out of the past. But this
is no relic, no museum piece.
See. This football is still in use,
staring back like an idol's head,
still worshipped now as much as then.

Injury Room

In here the blue and white is clinical,
the smell of antiseptic's headed in,
proof our heroes too are blood and muscle,
like the pumping of the ice machine,
Savlon wound wash, pre-injection swabs,
insect repellent, Nivea after sun,
reclining beds that could hold poolside gods,
Keane, Kanoute, Redknapp, Anderton.
This piece of White Hart Lane is sacred ground,
like that other stadium at Delphi,
whose oracle shows things can turn around.
We've protectors who will grant us victory.
Bill Nicholson is our talisman.
The Spurs cockerel heralds a new dawn.

Defoe

All he ever thinks about is football.
>   A maths teacher on Jermain Defoe

When strikes come in waves like breakers on deck,
you weather the storm and meet your match.
Stands foam with tension, released like a catch.
The toughest of the crew doubt you'll pull back
from the brink. You kneel after a tackle
before the great score board that makes and breaks,
arms outstretched. A Sky camera might mistake
a look of prayer for thanks after a goal.
But you're not repenting the route you chose,
not to set course by the maths teacher's word,
shooting off his received map of the world.
Only by adventure can a son lose
the travelled path so as then to find
the true score and green at the tunnel's end.

Keane

(after Heaney)

And sometime take the Central Line out east
to follow a hedgerow along Luxborough Lane
till you reach a training ground and field,
where players strike like October wind,

and a squad, divided like a cell developing,
shoots at shifted goalposts at close range,
so that you catch an Ireland international
getting past an England keeper's defence,

and as he leaves his signature, eyes
the colour of the ocean off County Clare
blow your heart, till you are leagues away
on the rock of another age and shore.

Audere Est Facere
To Dare is To Do

You can study the laws of physics,
balance equations of speed and spin,
take doctorates in aerodynamics,
or curl it like Keane and get it in.
You can analyse pattern in chaos,
predict the markets and Premiership,
trade in futures, referee torts,
or do as Kanoute and take a kick.
You can commentate on politics,
or be a player. You have a choice,
be a critic of Keats' iambics,
or pen your own and find your voice,
stand on the sidelines, despair, give up,
or risk it like Redknapp and bust a gut.

Tottenham Hotspur 1, Blackburn Rovers 0

The final score has a pleasing sound,
the Proustian rush of childhood weekends,
the storytime lilt of that voice on *Grandstand*,
a piano scale that climbs, then descends,

and after this the smell of a bonfire,
the dry ice mist of winter breath,
Pat Jennings and John Travolta,
the test card on a 3-channel TV set,

and certain knowledge that Saturday
is pay in the bank, not yet run down,
though Sunday, wearing Puritan grey,
will knock with homework to be done.

Captains

Everyone was talking about
Santini and Arnesen,
but the word might have been

of those other consuls,
Natalia and Angela
on the Club's reception,

high priests of information,
like the time Jamie had
all those stitches

and where Louise kissed him better,
or the good news
of their son's arrival,

keepers of Redknapp's royal trainers,
cased in their box like glass slippers,
size ten and white as a saint.

Late News

Archaeologists have unearthed a hoard
of silverware in the northern district
of the area formerly known as London.
The treasure trove, which dates from
2,000 years ago, was found on the site
of the Tottenham Hotspur Football Club.
Findings confirm the cultural importance
of the game in early 21st-century life and
the dominant position held by the Club.
The friendly competition of football
was in stark contrast to the hostilities
which shook the world later that century.
The sport was played by a social élite.
Fragments of decorated drinking vessels
were discovered adjacent to the hoard.
Such was the prestige attached to players,
it is believed men were buried in their kit.

Goal

Start from space, with planets in formation
on the football pitch of the universe,
the back four, Sun, Mercury, Venus, Earth,
midfield of Mars, Jupiter and Saturn,
with strikers, Uranus, Neptune, Pluto,
not chilling, but playing for our galaxy
in an interstellar soccer fantasy.
Zoom in until you see our spinning globe,
as though a foot had touched it in midair.
Move closer till somewhere over London
you spot the Tottenham Hotspur stadium.
Focus on the path of our human sphere,
kicked this way and that, as if at random.
Now watch how life rewards goal-led action.

In Memoriam Sidney Wells

You're driving down Lordship Lane
aged fourteen in your first car.
It's the year of Stanley Baldwin
and *Yes We Have No Bananas*.
You don't yet know your wife,
the two children who miss you
still more with the years, how life
will stall before you're through.
You won't live long enough to meet
your only grandchild,
but now I'm walking down your street.
Three weeks before you die
you'll choose to come back.
An estate will be here, the house gone,
though this won't cause the heart attack.
Rather, like geese, you'll want to fly home.
Leaving, you'll return where you were born.

Against Metaphor

Here Pompey means Portsmouth.
There is no Caesar, or Caesarean.
We're singing because we've won 3-1,
but the landslide isn't literal
and we're on firm ground.

This is not a paddock. The players
are neither trophies nor horseflesh.
This green field is not a scientific pun,
a *Secret Garden* or Sandford Park.
Nor is it the exile of Tiberius.

We're Tottenham till we die,
but no one's being buried here today.
This turf is not the Somme.
Santini's gone, but still alive.
Programmes are not manifestos or hymns.

Police who tell opposition stands to sit
aren't prefects, teachers or Nazis,
or Marxists up the corridor at work.
That angry teenager is not led away
yet. A gull is free to circle and to fly.

Our bodies packed in stands are not
battery hens or meat to feed to cannons.
Slow feet shuffle back to the weekend,
not morning lessons. A sign reads
'Spurs' in the community, not 'care'.

The icon on its orb is not a crucifix.
A cockerel isn't crowing three times.
Here character doesn't lead to tragedy
and human heroism is life not art.
We're in White Hart Lane, not heaven,

though in myth heaven is a place like this.
And this thing we're willing away
from the open posts of our goal
is neither a bomb nor a baby,
but sweet FA, only a bloody ball.

Kabul

In Kabul's athletics stadium
where a crowd of children, women and men
condoned through communal inaction
the Taleban's first public execution
of a woman, a mother of seven,

and watched the spectator sport of a spirit
smothered by the blanket excuse of a bullet,
sending up a medieval shout of 'God is great',
girls are now playing football and celebrate
on concrete sidelines, shooting at fate.

By Hart

Seeing the European Cup won
for Liverpool, England, Britain,
a euphoria that breaks barriers,
a naked release of inhibition,
the energy of evidence scoring
intimacy, outreach, gladness,

I'm filled with longing for the Lane,
a tribe's contagious madness,
the proximity of agreement,
vocal alliance of the crowd,
multiplying the collective mind,
wearing its heart out loud,

magnifying New Year's Eve,
a peace march, a General Election,
into a stadium of citizens, enthused
in concert with primal celebration,
raising souls of Heysel, Hillsborough,
through human regeneration.

At White Hart Lane

Waiting for a train this winter evening,
as a distant siren calls and fallen rain
reflects still swings, a red bus makes
progress into the future, and something
like a comet or prophecy from *Macbeth*,
or the cockerel on a weather vane,

moves for North London, pointing
in the direction of the wind, speaking
words of Dylan, telling of a ruler's fall,
when Stamford Bridge next comes to
White Hart Lane. The tournament at
Old Trafford revealed ill-gotten gain is

no substitute for the true score crossing
the line. Some things can't be bought
but go deeper, like a father and son now,
walking along Love Lane. Tonight's tempest
brings voices and stands singing, 'The Club
for England, Hotspur and their King'.

X POEMS

Easter X
March 2005
(for Gonga)

I

I'd not registered how the empty church
opposes the ground, like a hulk or shell,
its entombed dust abandoned like burial,
a stark contrast to the living work
as crowds manifest for the match and swell.
I'm with Jol's army, not graveyard silence,
but White Hart Lane's saving ambulance,
England's Red Cross, the order of St John,
the security of uniformed policemen,
sirens singing, a fire engine's salvation,
Spurs' cockerel crowing with each new sun,
as Jol hatches goals and plans for Tottenham,
where players who fall climb back on
and light breaks through an open Pantheon.

II

The drum roll builds over Spurs' sound system.
We're chanting a rain dance like a Baptist hymn,
'standing up in the pouring down',
visited with cheer like a Madness song.
So much depends on alliteration,
the YES of Spurs versus the F of Fulham,
the need to ride again, not be mummified,
to spring like March from a coffin and rise,
the heart's White Hart winning its heat,
Defoe's determination to dominate,
lashing out of hooves, kicks from Kanoute,
Keane's shots begetting Yeats' 'terrible beauty',
Robinson's saves diffusing German bombs,
delivering us with St Paul's protection.

III

Next day in the Imperial War Museum
I visit the Great Escape Exhibition,
not for asylum, though this was once Bethlem,
but to see how men headed straight for freedom
under the blackout of a March New Moon,
glided free from Colditz and its concrete prison
to Canadas and Englands of the imagination.
I remember stepping from a white van
with my hands up, ripping up a Section form,
as a hospital tore up my right to freedom,
a squad of nurses invading a room,
issuing a needle like an ultimatum,
because I refused to swallow poison,
then rising early to pace the grounds alone.

IV

In this Sunday museum I see traces of men
like the Spurs before who go marching on
in the squad's new blood, their names emblazoned
as on scholarship boards, or village stones,
ghost photos of writers who tunnelled with tin,
built corridors from power, exited tombs.
I see tapestry legions and armies of sperm
sacking Troy, Red missiles lodged like Masons,
a Turk's bullet shot in my grandfather's side,
like a planted tree of death, not life.
And suddenly I see the Rose Croix,
on the Wooden Horse men rose from under
and at last translate it, not as something sinister,
but as clear and bright as David's Star.

V

I remember the Oxford synagogue, friendlier
than any church, the words 'Rebecca' and 'Sarah'
written in Scripture, like the Mosquito's cheer
I'd pass with my grandmother at RAF Stanmore.
And I see a cross can represent, not death,
not murder, not nails, not bombs, but release,
not bowing in Mass, but a mass Exodus,
not Caesar stabbed, or C-section, but Genesis,
how OT is Oedipus Rex and Old Testament,
Papal keys can lock or unlock a continent,
that St Christopher and the child he carries
are Ascanius, Aeneas and Anchises,
the Trinity and all mythologies of Casaubon
are a phoenix, Osiris and 9/11.

VI

And a cockerel is crowing like three knocks to a door,
not nails in a cross, but a summons to a Chamber,
not breaking and entering, but permission to open,
not the drive of a car bomb, but a Word programme,
and I'm seeing what happens beyond veil and screen,
in Oxford's Apollo and Cambridge's Newton,
what teenage boys' whispers conveyed in the Union,
a crossing of the Orange Lodge and Sinn Féin,
Eleusinian mysteries in the Temple of Solomon,
the Sphinx transubstantiating to brotherhood's man,
not a gang rape of Mary, but a goal and delivery
from war to peace, bomb to birthday, ceasefire to treaty,
not Athene's or Sparta's humiliation,
but a plague and state cured through life's translation.

VII

Words are lambswool for Theseus and Ariadne,
leading to crossroads from crosswords of enemies,
the one across, one down clues for community,
the *pax* that a sporting defeat makes with victory,
fresh air theatre, spectator therapy,
the Great Escape from attack or surgery,
the will of Antigone surviving through family,
tackling and passing on mortality.
In the museum a couple play a game,
telling their toddlers to speak their names,
not letting them pass till they utter the code,
like sentries guarding a lifelong road,
and the children giggle like one on trial
in a driving test, wedding, exam, Cup Final.

VIII

In Bethnal Green at the *Spit Lit* festival,
writers are debating conflicts of difference,
religion, race, gender and critical schools.
I see the festival logo dividing like cells,
saying *Split It*, meaning the difference, the madness,
till diversity reduces to human interest.
At work a lecturer in culture and media
erects a white on black, black on white poster,
'Research isn't terrorism' in capital letters,
the final word encased in barbed wire.
More and more I see that mania
is a diagnosis for group behaviour,
less a term for dissenting characters,
than for PhDs, doctors, dividers-and-rulers.

IX

St Jol is a born again Joan of Arc,
riding before each man to meet Pompey
or fire at the Gunners. He takes the flak,
doesn't pass the buck, and holds the baby.
But after the game, who gets the gold mark?
All of King's men share defeat or victory.
The scales share out praise and blame, loss and luck.
The Club is many, the head and body.
Jol is on track to be the new Bill Nick,
but even the coach carries on learning.
Don't cross to Ajax, or do as he did
and fall on a sword of your own making,
or burn on a funeral pyre which you lit.
Show them the management's not for turning.

X

White Hart Lane's a globe, a spinning ball,
and all her team are worldly players.
There is the turnstile and the tunnel.
A man in his time may be striker and manager,
being and not being always the future,
escaping with kit willingly to shoot,
hammering home the score like a lover,
always the warrior, Keane to the hilt,
till a petition fills Justice's gown,
the point is given and scales start to fill,
like a simnel cake rising, a baker's eleven,
with each signing heading and kicking at goal
on the birthing pitch, testing iambic feet,
in training for next season's final minute.

To an Ex-OUCA President

*(in the year of Margaret Thatcher's 80th birthday
and 30th anniversary of her election as Tory leader)*

Remember, remember the traitors' duplicity,
when the Mother of Parliament faced disloyalty
and Britannia was knifed in the womb of democracy,
as white brethren repudiated matriarchy
with collective ingratitude and insanity,
though she'd steered their party to electoral victory
with a love-hate mandate from her country,
fertile policies and ideology,
diplomatic and military agility,
lack of hesitancy, and firm tenacity.

Recall the spirit of aim and accuracy,
the Eighties obsession with strict efficiency,
as if no enterprise could be done sufficiently
without concentration kept up continuously,
and the PM were part of her own constituency,
one Puritan among a greater majority,
contributing to the gross domestic economy,
according to the pragmatic philosophy
of diversification and the strict formality
of effort, timesheets and accountability.

With the turning of the globe and the new century
self-regard and reliance gained reciprocity
in an era of rational spirituality,
a time for both family and charity,
when each sees he, or she, is at liberty
to lay claim to his, or her, emotional territory,
to inhabit his, or her, intellectual property,
in order to be one among a body of many,
a soldier in the onward human army,
an ally of live striving and humility.

Some dauntless Thatcher with the same facility
for helmsmanship, who values similarly
freedom to act and achieve, yet also liberty
from oppression socially, politically,
and, identifying with Mother Earth, ecologically,
will in time step onto the stage and radically
transform the lie of the land, so in every locality
citizens will realise they belong to a justly
ordered society, where opportunity
can be sought by persons equally but differently.

For the self which, like a tortoise, you carry
on your back, bearing with yourself, is the duty
to survive and pass on through the ceremony
of life experience, which consequently
others may copy, so that ownership privately
is not solely surroundings and any plenty
with which you dwell, but ultimately
and more importantly the necessary
conditions of life as well, from the unity
of *habeas corpus* to relations publicly.

So value the ethics of equal diversity,
individual and social responsibility,
the business of corporate sustainability,
taxation of energy, thought and industry,
moral and marketplace multiplicity,
a perspective of feminist femininity,
outlooks and skills of the new plurality,
the enterprise of free will and ability,
holistic health and the global community,
the full spectrum of innovative humanity.

Ex-prospective

(after Hogarth)

A whitewashed think tank rolls along Whitehall,
advertising a strong, improved leader
with airbag, a boy in a thought bubble

camouflaged as a people carrier
on a platform behind bulletproof glass,
with pop politics on the loudspeaker

blaring, while crowds wave the Popemobile past.
A guard on the Scottish Office roof sees
a grassy knoll lurks in St James's Park.

A virus is detected, a file cleaned.
But which is first, the Yard or the rooster?
In the dug-out there's a management team

watching and listening with big brother,
spotting the ball, predicting market trends,
busy plotting fall guys, transfers, futures.

Words, words, words caught by invisible hands
are saved on disc and taped off the record
by men parked at the helm of unmarked vans.

The vehicle for change is a coach and scores
goals for and points with the electorate,
making progress in the table, love not war,

broadcasting 'Cool Britannia' on the state
of the art system, as a dalek arm,
aimed at voters, sprays policies like paint,

its antenna, or Leviathan limb,
reaching out to find sense and press the flesh,
as if laws of the land, and attraction,

have been released from a muzzle and leash.
There's a street Party, popping bulbs and pills,
as groups focus and Damascus lights flash.

The field's as level as a ref's whistle,
but here come the key players from the wings,
cabinet, closet and through the tunnel.

The game kicks off with everyone diving
and ducking together in Britart beds.
The Members' club dancefloor is for crossing,

as public and private sectors bash heads
and jump float in a funeral procession
or parody of empire, long since dead.

For this is the carnival of Britain,
a christening of the common interest.
Welfare, profit, press and politicians

do mergers and get on down to business.
Reserves are in the bank and on the bench.
How the roadshow goes is anyone's guess,

or who'll be in at Numbers One and Ten,
when right is divined at the final count
and the Long Parliament comes to an end.

Later, red-eyed but blue-tied from his round
of red phones, red flags, red boxes to mug,
red lights on air, wired with tea and for sound

the one with the mandate they'll hate and love,
hounded like a fox in a master's coat,
with red and blue, old and New, in his blood

will work out the percentage of the vote,
labouring late at night over the shop
with the light on, loving every minute,

the whole lock, stock, enterprise and Starship,
the think tank and thinking outside the box,
while at the same time remaining in it.

X: A Poetry Political Broadcast

I

Welcome back for our election special.
Now a news report could be a found text.
But can politicians prove their metal

and pass poetry's lie detector test?
Do they stand for clarity and vision,
or obfuscate? Where do we place the stress?

Consciousness evolved so each equation,
written on the blackboard of the brain's eye,
can be worked through to the right solution

relative to situation and time.
Ideas are loopholes out of the default
programme, which sets a reflex party line.

Our species must adapt or else we'll halt
at the first crossroads and stick in a rut.
But our imaginations let us vault

to possible savannahs. We jump-cut
to other scenes, as we extrapolate
futures of bonds before the markets shut.

We listen to both sides of a debate,
as Reds move for the heart, Blues for the head.
Views circulate like blood. We legislate

by majority, but can be misled
by the riddles of so-called plain-speaking.
In our Communication Age we're fed

the belief all rhetoric is cheating,
that oratory and poetry lack proof.
But if it's integrity you're seeking,

you'll find it in poems, not spin. In youth
we know verse is *sound* and voices sixth sense.
This is a documentary about truth.

II

Take this couple here, sitting on the fence
before the *News at Ten*'s chattering class,
as the anchor plays Speaker and attempts

to keep order, let kids reply or ask
a question in Westminster's bumptious school.
Our couple watch each politician's mask

slip like a tragic reversal and peel
to bare-faced ambition lying beneath.
Public interest conceals a private goal.

And so the seed is sown that words lack truth,
that there's a gap between what's said and meant,
and nothing but nothing is sworn on oath.

Our couple question each other's intent.
What's truth or love? Is anything constant
in a democracy of flux and rent?

Sky-high disinterest and ideals of Kant
fall like twin towers on their TV screen.
Print columns in *The Times* or tabloids rant,

multiplying and magnifying spleen
towards those who sin, or are sinned against.
What meaning's left? What is there left to mean?

Paralysed by this existential angst,
they see photographs of a limbless boy,
or the statue of Ozymandias,

as Saddam is toppled, like a tin toy.
And if truth exists, where does truth reside?
Who'll redistribute it to *hoi polloi*?

Or is the truth in fact that truth has died,
along with romance, the author and god?
Are we drifting with no breeze on the tide?

III

What swells our sails? What replaces the rod
of the old religions, which demand love
as divine right, define truths as paths trod,

and shroud each mysterious chess-board move
in clouds of tautology? Politicians
at least make a show of trying to prove

and to justify their own positions,
but other ministers hide behind faith
and altars, where moral obligations

are forced from packs like a magician's ace,
where each IS transubstantiates to OUGHT,
and each coffin's corpse sublimates to wraith.

Far better to steer your own ship of thought,
let poetry fill your sail, than canvass
or follow the fleet. Ideas that are wrought

in your workshop, as you breathe globes in glass,
and clay that's fired in the kiln of your brain
have more value, because you're your own boss,

with no interpreter or middleman.
The truth is we are motivated most
by those carrots we ourselves imagine.

A rendez-vous in the heavenly host,
and myth of marriage for eternity,
are better PR than hell's Sunday roast.

You can kneel down before authority,
drowned by the conditioning system's noise,
or listen to that quiet clarity

as you tune to the wavelength of your voice.
Switch on the light bulb of poetic truth,
or stay in the dark age. It's a free choice.

IV

Our couple, under their covers and roof,
lie together. The truth is they're apart.
It takes courage to know you're your own root

and branch, your own finishing line and start.
And is this all? Can this be all there is?
She hears the mechanism of his heart

regulating his body as he breathes,
sees their eyes and skeletons stripped by time,
sockets robbed, like radios by car thieves.

It seems to her she's a production line.
The latest model revs beneath her hood,
as her unborn son stirs like an engine.

And she knows the child will come to no good.
Today he may slumber deep in her womb,
but one day he'll sleep in a coffin's wood.

She dreams of fields cradling men on the Somme.
Her soundtrack falls silent for a minute.
She contemplates space, wonders if there's room

for yet another death on the planet,
if all the berths are reserved or taken,
if the shuttle sells a return ticket,

and where on earth is the destination
anyway. She hopes it is Adlestrop,
or that station from *The Railway Children*.

But this train is direct and doesn't stop
to look back. It speeds through history faster,
leaves Battle's crossed swords on an OS map

for two hundred years after Trafalgar,
Guy Fawkes' four hundredth anniversary
and the diamond of Hiroshima.

V

It seems we're on target for entropy,
that the truth is darkness, but just ahead
the universe shows signs of poetry,

of making and expansion. Light is shed,
but what mysteries does poetry make clear?
That's easy. The mazes from which we're led

by poetry are the choices we fear.
She's the *daimon* solving our dilemmas
in questions of survival, love and war,

where taking one road means other vistas
will be fenced off from our paths forever.
At the X of each crossroads she appears,

like Venus as Aeneas' protector.
As though from a retiring room, she's there
to favour one or other barrister

and tip the balance. She is Athena
with a casting vote to free or damn.
She's as articulate as Medea,

but benign as the invisible hand
of *laissez-faire*. The Sistine Chapel
would show her, not reaching, but touching man.

She's the Russian dolls inside each fractal,
Darwin's and Dawkins' Mother Nature,
the quirk or quark that predicts each petal

adds up to a Fibonacci number.
She's the fulcrum point of an equation,
a planetarium that's a mirror

image of the brain writ large, an action
perfected in the grace of Greek sculpture,
or lover's pulse echoed by an ocean.

VI

Geneticists may find the elixir,
when the codes are written and the book read.
The question then may follow the answer.

We'll multiply the living by the dead,
times all our tens of millions of brain cells
by waves that have smashed against Beachy Head,

divide the stars by the sum of black holes,
or human bones by our three score and ten,
calculate to recurring decimals

the probability words of madmen
contain the kernel of internal truth,
that history's comet will again return,

like a calendar's days, the way June 6th
raised ghosts of the Normandy invasions
before the vote in Europe on June 10th.

But for now we'll use our X-ray vision
to translate emotion in people's heads
from the common language of expression,

as we unearth conflicting scripts and texts.
What sets us apart from other species
is our attraction to all things complex.

Humans explore continents and theories,
work out infinite equations for X,
examine possible worlds and histories,

explicate atoms, pull the thorns that vex.
We extrapolate from experience,
plot the future's graph with each pencilled X.

We're missiles seeking meaning, order, sense.
Both rocket scientists and pacifists
have learnt right angles and the perfect tense.

VII

Plato thought those entrusted with office
should have PhDs in logic and maths.
But I believe prose breeds only sophists

and government figures disguise the truth.
Was it really poetry's emotion
that bothered him, or his own need for warmth?

Although he idolised the blinding sun,
he imitated the cool of his cave.
Forster's *Only connect* wouldn't have done.

Platonic dreams look, but don't misbehave.
Sidney saw poetry can please and teach,
and on the confident crest of a wave

the grandiose conclusion Shelley reached
was that poets are the legislators
time forgot. Poetry can reform speech.

Its branches of thought are propagators
of fresh growth, like leaves of a tree, book, bill,
leaving instructions to executors,

bequeathing both a motive and a will.
Irrelevance is the antithesis
of poetry. Far from ineffectual,

she is a strong, active voice. *Poiesis*
can cook up ideas from next to nothing.
She's the synthesis of thought and *praxis*.

I like to think if Plato were writing
now, he'd see Forms as Icons on the screen,
not otherworldly, but the hard-wiring

innate to thought, the host in the machine.
Plato gets the benefit of the doubt,
my phone-in vote for the form of my dreams.

VIII

Think how the X with which you mark your vote
is less a symbol of affirmation,
than a *No*, like a noughts-and-crosses stroke.

We are led more by the motivation
to keep one gang out than choose the other.
It's the politics of opposition,

the X of exclusion and of danger.
X marks the spot. It's a skull and crossbones,
or enmity towards an ex-lover.

Witness the irony of chromosomes
which spell the oppression of half the race:
a double X bars a woman's options,

as if doors slam twice as hard in her face.
Picture women like so many cattle,
branded with the X of a husband's name.

Conjure the sign on a map for battle,
the X of crossed swords where men died and clashed
over disputes we still try to settle,

the treasure chests of women, land and cash.
We all reach a crossroads where four roads meet.
Some of us will take a wrong turn or crash,

some will push ahead up a one-way street,
or go with what they know the route they came,
while turning-points help others to their feet.

Though a pack of XXXX can be to blame,
happiness is choice. It's filling your cup,
deciding how to play your hand, or game.

Buy a party line and you're sold a pup
The only crime is that of indifference.
Better lose your mind, than not make it up.

IX

And so I speak in poetry's defence.
Whenever we face the X of a blank,
it's the poet in us all that attempts

to conjure the answer. It's her we thank
for each idea, image, new line to take.
She defrags files in our memory bank,

reshuffles our cabinet and can make
a big bang from the dreams of sleep's abyss.
As you lie in the bath, she's by a lake

fishing for a wreck in your subconscious,
locating hoards with a divining rod,
dredging legends from Lethe, or Loch Ness.

She's a privatised muse, or public God.
To me she's the current in the machine,
the self-selecting song on the iPod,

the translation that says what brain states mean.
She's what's missing from a scan or X-ray:
of this world, not the next, or in between.

She's the frequency found when people pray,
when they walk, write or paint, dance, solve or sing,
the concentration where things fall away

and you're on the stimulant of being.
Is it any wonder she tells the truth?
It's wrong to think poetry's misleading

and remote. It's prose that's cold and aloof,
makes the weaker argument seem stronger,
and talks at, and down to, you from his brief.

Prose is a bombast who boxes clever,
but poetry's the voice inside your head,
the rhyme and reason, the muse and measure.

X

Now picture an assembly of the dead.
and those not yet born. How much would they give
to be here choosing in your shoes instead?

A life of making is a life well lived.
It's harder for all the dead to return
than to pass each grain of sand through a sieve.

So what are the conclusions we have learned?
We all support the Poetry Party.
Membership isn't bought, withdrawn or earned.

Her manifesto is autonomy.
Abstain from her and you abstain from life.
This is the truth behind democracy.

Dictators watch begging bowls queue for rights,
burn the names on an electoral roll.
Women are hidden out of mind and sight.

Poetry's pleasure is comparable
to pushpin, Bentham said. Then are labour
pains like growing ones? It's defensible

is it to kill, or to bomb the lesser
of two human shields? And if you change track
to hit the smaller and miss the larger,

does this qualify as a moral act?
Double effect, double talk or whammy?
Sexing, faxing or fucking up the facts?

Filter the waste of postmodernity,
politics' white noise, theory's doublespeak.
Set course by the Pole Star of poetry,

like a ship of state. Discern true from fake.
XX or XY are rolls of the die,
but each kiss, vote, mark is a choice we make.

SHEET MUSIC

Independence Day Dawn
4th July 2005

(for Jonathan Charles Haynes)

There are as many pebbles on a beach
as sonnets, both composed and yet unmade,
as many blades of wild grass out of reach
as pipes of Pan and songs which could be played,
as many starfish closing up their eyes
as opening rays, as moon hands to sun,
as many crystals and fireflies
as inlet rocks, where sea responds to stone.
So let fluidity converse with still,
July show surprise insect candlelight,
constellations be joined by heaven's quill
and dawn chorus descants unite in right.
And as you walk along a stretch of shore,
pocket a sonnet, pebble, blade, song-score.

Footprints

Here on a beach outside Liverpool
millennia of mudflats wash away,
peeling time's face pack to a summer day
five thousand years ago. Empires rose and fell

like layers of deposit and the sea level,
and now in this quiet Lancashire bay
Stone Age footprints tell more than flint can say.
See him run, his prints deeper at the ball,

striding at a speed of three miles per hour,
as he hunts, or herds, a red roe deer,
whose hooves skid in sand, whilst over there
women's footprints show the hunter's gatherers

beachcombing for shellfish, and this way and that
run the smaller steps of children's tracks,
mudlarking as the breeze answers back.
Soon their marks will be wiped to a clean slate,

but for the length of a play they speak once more,
writing a scene which history tore
from its books, told first round a wood hut's fire,
now written by foot on a northern shore.

Hackney Downs

Tonight there's red sky over Hackney Downs,
a sign of good weather tomorrow,
shepherd's delight, the saying used to go,
before sheep were driven out of town,

and the city's tide put all this under water.
Soon darkness will cry an ocean for the dying,
someone's father will be leaving, someone's lying,
someone's son using someone's daughter,

someone's mother reaching the refuge centre.
But now the sunset, like a pipe, says *Listen*
to a man beneath his CD walkman,
to a married woman whose head is covered,

to some who believe, some who aren't believers.
I see the same washing lines on balconies,
the same low-rise estates, converted factories.
I hear a call go dead on a receiver

and then the possible horizon singing.
The train gallops on to London Fields.
This piece of land was once light years BC
and somewhere on it there were shepherds watching.

After London

After hostilities were declared,
after the chemical warfare,
after the carrying out of the dead
and the deaths of those who carried,
when the stench of all that was rotten
in the lapsed state had blown away,

April lilacs sprang from the earth,
thistles seized trimmed lawns and parks,
parliaments of crows sat in recess,
starlings formed their own assemblies,
dandelion clocks took possession
of cracks in government buildings,

foxes claimed deserted blocks,
sheep and cattle went on the march,
evergreens put down roots
in row after row of borough streets,
strays looted vacant shops,
ivy gripped Centre Point,

the London Eye overturned,
gales brought the BT tower down,
Canary Wharf began to lean,
Nelson's column crumbled like a Roman ruin,
salmon swam in the freshwater Thames
and banks were exchanged for mudflats again.

Sheet Music

What are we and the world but shored-up thoughts
written in fossil evidence,
a backing track of double helices and strings,
revolving on axes of desire,
inner cores of change at beats per revolution,
eras per second,
the ascent of man a scale beyond ultrasound,

the very ground we stand on
shifting, gifting us with new selves, opening rifts
between true and magnetic north,
conjoining mind and body, making mountains
out of atoms, turning plates
like pages to sheet music, to vibrations of earthquakes
in the lie of the land,

hot air rising, grievances erupting like rain or fallout,
unstable metals conducting
the symphony of energy to boiling and vanishing point,
skidding off the graph,
skating over paper ice, falling from the lid of a flat earth
down black hole chutes
into a volcanic abyss, zero gravity, where laws are liquid

for matter as for morals,
mutable as the identity of nations, continents colliding
like dodgems
or molecules of oil walking on water, a people
leaving Egypt
or nomads on the move in Africa, land masses
fitted in a jigsaw,

each cell raising the sea level and temperature,
certain of nothing
but drift, of hitting Ground Zero running, of migrations
of geese and men,
that our Western *terra firma* was once desert, rainforest,
at the equator before us,
and of the rock music which plays beneath our feet?

Baggage

I've seen the Winged Victory in the Louvre
and Thierry take the cup at White Hart Lane,
caught Venus Rising from her oyster
twenty years ago in the window of a train,

glimpsed the Reclining Buddha in Bangkok
and my lover sleeping in a Gatwick dawn,
taken a banana plane from Barbados
and landed in the open arms of Paddington,

traversed the Hellespont and Rubicon,
entered Livingstone's congestion zone,
stood on the Areopagus in Athens
and in the Commons, hearing Divisions echo,

read the roll-call at the Menin Gate
and survival in a Hampstead mother's sons,
witnessed a plaque by Hungary's Parliament,
Romania's rebirth in a Westminster baptism,

asked Apollo at Delphi for asylum
and the Priory Hospital to be released,
made a pilgrimage to the Vatican
and Sunday shopping centre at Brent Cross,

cruised below the Golden Gate Bridge
and down to Electric Avenue,
shot the Colorado River rapids
and a glance in Bar Italia's rear-mirror view,

tripped to the libraries at Ephesus
and St Pancras, looking for a question,
answered in The Thinker's paralysis
and this night bus, screening my own reflection.

English Civil War

Above the valley woods wait like armies,
lining the brow of the opposing hills.
Trees deliver loose leaf ultimatums,
'Cede, or fall', carried on the breeze.
In the basin they are not a warlike people.
A sea of wheat surrounds their peaceable land.
Barbed wire brambles mark their borders.
In summer gardens, grapes hang on wisteria vines.
Foxglove tassles are the height of fashion.

Red hot poker players are gambling for time.
In underground cells the enslaved soil plots,
sowing insurrection on the storms of change.
Plants are smuggled in. The armoured oak
and the first brave saplings start to shoot.
The old garden order begins to choke.
The forests are demanding room to expand.
Acorn grenades hang, ready to explode.
Pampas bayonets stab at the dusk sky.

Premonition

Which pub were we walking back from that night?
I can't remember, can recall only this,
the huge industrial cylinder end of the moon
like an altar cloth at the top of factory lines
of low-rise blocks, bone ivory as a key
sounding the first notes of Debussy's
menstrual memory, how we fumbled with the lock,
and crept upstairs, and as we passed her door,
I sensed our daughter dream, and in the afterglow
dreamt myself that she tracked a river-bed which cut
through the park we tell her not to walk in
after dark, that it led her onto an infamous estate
where an ancient celebrity once lived,
Artemis or Ceres or Hecate,
that she was drawn by prison bars of sheet music
playing in the castle grounds of her subconscious,
sleepwalking in a white cotton nightdress,
not the candyfloss pink one with Justin on it,
and came at last to a clearing in a forest,
where an alabaster statue of the goddess,
a soft porn sculpture, stood at the heart of a maze,
trimmed by levellers, whose scythes lay in wait,
propped up against the pedestal with rakes,
that I shouted after her, but she couldn't hear,
that she was lost without the thread of a meaning,
a tourist in another country,
throwing bread away like currency,
like loaves and fishes, into a Roman fountain,
as if we hadn't taught her the value of money,
and that her lunar beauty was reflected
in the newly minted silver of its surface,
a coined empress, till she ends up in the sack
with the toad, who squats at the water's edge.

Breakthrough

The Easter before finals I suffered madness,
which ancient Greeks ascribed to the womb
wandering round the body's wilderness,
fleeing from its proper function.

I'll always remember my own resistance,
when I thought I was Mary crossed with Christ,
the Holy Spirit raping me in darkness,
and how I punched my stomach with my fist.

Noli Me Tangere

(after U.A. Fanthorpe and Titian)

I

Poor innocent, don't you want me to save you?
I always loved you with a passion. Your disciples
plotted for world dominion, but your touch,
Mr Fall Guy, was healing, a laying on of hands,
your body heaven. 'Take, eat and don't forget me,'
you said the last time. Now you tease me, censor
your own visions, a limbless tree, lost to a dead-end
wilderness of sand, deserting your inner god. I am
not your mother, son, nor was meant to be. See
the distant town, the one true way it enjoys secular
sin, the flock breeding in a green shade. Your name
will live for ever, but will you once? They know not
what they do and most don't ask, for there's no answer,
only an urgent imperative. Life's a joke, gone too fast.

II

Down, girl. Sit and stay. You're no longer fit
to wash my feet. Don't you know who I've become?
I'm the three-in-one, special, going for an evensong,
a riddle's answer: infant, adult, old man.
In my Pampers shroud I'm born-again. I flash
my flesh like a revelation, a dormitory pin-up
for monkish habits, calendar boy, Mr April. I always rise
from the tomb and bear my rod, this prophet's staff,
like death's scythe. Behold my wounds. I'm a new man,
renaissance enough to save a whore from certain death,
but not to let her touch me, take my godlike powers,
steal my hardwon soul. I'm Superman but Clark Kent
has limits. I've been whipped, pinned to a cross.
What more do you ask of me? Must I come again?

Sarah Malcolm in Prison

(William Hogarth, National Gallery of Scotland, Edinburgh)

You look away to your left, arms folded,
avoiding eye contact with the artist, as with
constable, magistrate, priest. Those rosary beads
on the table are worn with prayers, petitions
for your case to be reheard. They echo
in Newgate now like last supper screams.

But you're no scarecrow martyr and won't
be hung for a murder as for a lamb, committed
to innocence on that score, though marked
for slaughter. Your dignity is intact
even in the face of the sentence of death,
of that slammed and slatted door.

Despite your show of penitence and a last act
of remorse you'll stage in the cart to the gallows,
because your life then could depend on it, hanging
in the balance, you feel no regret for the woman
and her attendants, or the murderer who roped
you in, destroyer of faith, who left after the act,
deserting you for pieces of silver, the tankard
they found lodged in your rooms.

You're sorry only that justice has miscarried
and love aborted, that the wages of trust are debt,
for you've seen man face to face,
through the bottom of a glass, darkly,
tried him and found him wanting.

The revelation came sudden as sun in court,
as you attained appreciation of how killing
is possible, how you'd gladly have taken an axe
to the tallest of them there and then
and cleared a path to the light.

Your feeling is strong as the muscles on your arms
they claim can kill, as the resolve you hide well
but, like a knife, could stick in your gaoler,
their brothers' keeper,
as if hammering home a first nail.

Hymn to Enlightenment

Because stubborn men insist two plus two is three.
Because Father Christmas isn't up the chimney.
Because I'm warmed by the risen sun, not gloomy stalls.
Because I'm neither one of the elect, nor guilty of the fall.
Because it's a free country and I stand by my choice.
Because not even in psychosis have I ever heard a voice.
Because Zeus came before the holy ghost.
Because I didn't watch Robert Powell fake it on a cross.
Because Socrates was put to death before Jesus.
Because the resurrection is metaphor and myth.
Because masochism and ritual don't do it for me.
Because when my kin die, there'll not be signs made over their bodies.
Because I've never lacked a real person to whom to turn.
Because the herd smokes, gets pierced ears and confirmed.
Because that is wine and bread and I'm not a cannibal.
Because – repeat after me – this is a cloth and silver on a table.
Because intuition and intellect say a life goes out like a light.
Because my grandfather died when I was five.
Because turning the other cheek isn't always adaptive.
Because missionaries prey on the frail and false hope is addictive.
Because religious intolerance launches hate like a missile.
Because spiritual creeds are tools of secular control.
Because the Church is as corrupt as any other institution.
Because the Pope ordains male priests and backstreet abortions.
Because I have a Mother as well as a Father.
Because I don't talk to a man on a cloud, or ask heaven for answers.
Because I prefer the imagery of Athene and Mother Nature.
Because the ones who are living on are my grandmothers.
Because my mother revealed that 'God' was a word.
Because belief in the virgin birth and Turin shroud is absurd.
Because it's important to uphold truth and reason.
Because truth is to God as horse is to unicorn.
Because when outnumbered and nailed by needles, there's no love
        or mystery.
Because I've not lost faith in myself and human dignity.

Balance Sheet

And perhaps sometimes it evens out,
the lottery winner who was on the dole,
the blue-eyed choir boy abused by a priest,
the scholar bullied at boarding school,

the affair on a long-haul business trip,
the pretty girl talked into sex at twelve,
the playboy who can't form relationships,
the kept housewives who've lost themselves,

the athlete who grew up in foster care,
the bubbly, sociable alcoholic,
the band predicted to go nowhere,
the painter who is schizophrenic,

the heiress addicted to heroin,
the millionaire who once wore secondhand,
the president whose mother didn't love him,
the newborn son who wasn't planned.

Emily's Voice

*'I shall never marry, mother. It is one of the things I cannot
understand, how any woman who could live as a single woman
may live now in England, can not merely give up her freedom,
but merge her very individuality in that of another, and that
other too often one far inferior to herself. I would not do it for
any man that breathes!'*

*'The right man has not come yet, Helen,' said Mrs Wykeham,
with a smile.'*

E.M. ROACH, Dick Chichester;
or, the wooing of the county (1889)

Although November, the Cambridge postmark
brings hyacinths and harebells,
pushing life out of the dead earth.

This novel wrapped in white
is my grandmother's grandmother's
shroud or christening dress.

She speaks live down the line
in a voice I mistake
for prophecy or my own,

a Victorian engine hurtling downtrack
bearing genes, like coal
to fire theme and tone.

Indian Summer

Opening *The Times* the week after
you've turned ninety-nine, a feature
on a new drug from an ancient Chinese cure
brings to mind your cerebral malaria

and the quinine they gave you for your fever,
as your temperature hit a hundred and four
and went off the map that Indian summer
in the military hospital, where you bore

illness and my father, two months premature,
ten days before the Second World War,
when he broke out, as you lay in a coma
and you were both balancing on a high wire

as if the two of you might not now be here,
let alone me, whom later another doctor
would take by forceps from my mother,
the cord round me, like the noose of Jocasta.

Constance Ethelfleda

She is nursing, even now,
gnarled face smiling with sunlight,
bringing back from the dead
her younger brother. She hears,
comprehends. The rest is nightmare,
unfamiliar voices, faces, names,

legitimate wandering in memory,
worn with playing. The world
is turned upright, the cup reversing.
She shows us how to invert the V,
to mother, be mothered, feed, be fed,
to uphold dignity in birthing herself.

Frederick Maclean Wardle

You were not God or Father Christmas,
but a man in a Colonel Mustard cardigan
and blue eyes by a window onto a garden
where Giotto fed blackbirds in sunlight
and morning dew and our feet passed.

I was not Jesus and you were not Mary,
but I sat on your knee. You said
if I started an apple, I should finish it.
We ate cereal together round a table,
but it was breakfast, not the Last Supper.

The night you died, I sang you hymns.
Later they denied you a final injection,
bringing on the heart attack like thunder,
inducing death like birth, so the bed
would be clear for another's patience.

Next time I visited your house,
absence cored the air like a letter-knife.
No reply ever winged its way back.
I would sleep in your wife's twin bed.
I still see noughts and crosses in the beams,

wait for the Sandman to come like a
coffin lid to close, as *Jesus of Nazareth*
and adult talk I can't translate sweep in
from the living room and waves of music
and murder reach a fragile ascension.

Wards

My voice speaks out before me, breaks down
the silence that surrounds a ward bed.
In the corridor, footsteps away, you call,
'How did you know your dad's tread?'

We look into the common room, where
a Saturday film watches each patient's face,
then bunk off, like we're skiving lessons,
whistling the theme tune to *The Great Escape*.

Pacific Storm

In Kenting National Park
on the southernmost tip of Taiwan
I almost walked into the curtained web
of a spider the size of my hand,

but then from a vantage point,
like age or a plane's altitude,
I could see the terrain of rainforest,
like a mountain range or cloud,

and I thought as a storm was approaching,
like a fleet or a car wash brush,
that not even a three minute warning
heralds the first drop of madness.

Sea Views

A wave builds up, gathering momentum,
till it breaks on the shore, a burst bubble,
releasing white foam like sexual tension.

Café chairs touch feet beneath a table.
A waitress sighs. The backing track is slow.
A coffee cup cries a tear-stained dribble.

Like a Hobbema painting, tyre tracks go
in parallel from two points, y and x,
singly to infinity, like prints in snow.

Behind the counter a woman says, 'Next.'
A customer closes his umbrella.
A teenager sends and picks up a text.

I hear the stresses of the sea's metre,
crests that give and troughs that receive the thrust.
A heart should listen to its own writer.

A poem has to win the poet's trust.
'I offer you my hand,' I tell the page.
'Take it and the ocean will witness us.'

Covenant

As a *ketubah* marks more than marriage vows,
but paints the shades and colours of obligation,
and by its presence in the couple's house
sanctions their bond and promise like a god
or goddess of the hearth, I dreamt of a cloth,
like Peter seeing a sail, and of gathering wool
where it lay shed, combing it with a heckle,
dyeing it in the fleece, spinning each thread
on a bobbin, before weaving to life a tapestry
at a loom, like the weft and warp of this poem,
or like Penelope, no longer choosing to stall,
now the suitors are gone and Odysseus is home,
our minds entwined, as if together we were
strand and bodkin, or embroidered sampler.

Finding Space for Time

When we make love, like energy, we sprint
against a clock, an hour-glass hidden
in the mind and matter of existence,
so even now as we dash for freedom
across dimensions, we keep its promise,
do its bidding, prove the continuum
of a heart we can't define, but hear tick,
a baseline minim moving to the bomb
of innumerable big bangs, the script
of sperm, chalked sum of an equation,
proving the relativity of this
second, lover's distance, maker's baton,
where perspective collapses in
and negativity implodes to perception.

Schrödinger's Cat

So there I was, hovering over my corpse,
blinded by the light of an out-of-body experience,
enjoying the afterlife of a parallel universe,
done to death by phial like Romeo and Juliet,
after that photon zapped through the two-way mirror
and knocked over the poison sample like a skittle,

when in walks baldylocks, a Star Trekkie postdoc,
slightly the worse for beer, to unwrap the gift box,
and hazards the sight before his sore eyes is a cat,
that's not dead on arrival, but dozing on the mat,
not zipped up in black, but taking a siesta,
so *Time of death unknown* was entered later.

The Female Gaze

I write of arms and of a man,
arms that hold and a man
whose beauty is to be mute and gazed upon.
He is the silent movie star of this gallery.
Come with me through its halls.

Here he is framed naked from behind,
reclining on velvet, his face reflected in a mirror
held up by Cupid, watching me with a portrait's
moving eyes, as I appreciate his backside.
Observe him again as a young man, his skin
smooth and inviting, standing under a palm tree
in Tahiti in nothing but a sarong, offering
a bowl of ripe berries. Try one and see.

Notice him sitting in the European school.
Marvel at him on a piano stool,
his linen innocence, stiff sailor suit, blond curls.
Imagine teaching him duets. He is astonishing
as a Florentine model. And he can cook.
He grounds his lover when she levitates
too high on art. He strikes a pose for her, serene
as the Mona Lisa with a spliff. I like him best
as the god of youth, both arms missing,
his marble complexion that says he's spent
a life indoors at the loom, sheltered from the sun,
his waist slim, like a sapling that needs tending.

But I can be persuaded by his middle age,
flesh tumbling to the pull of gravity and empires,
his belly, a comfortable pillow, painted by Freud,
his shoulders strong enough to bear you.

And I can stare for hours at the nativity
of his daughter, his eyes cast down lovingly
in wonder, inviting us to linger on his face
for longer than an average glance might take,
without the feeling he'll look up and catch
our eyes fixated on him, gazing back.

Elegy

(for Michael Donaghy)

I left the self-help shelves in Waterstones
and US slang, sensing no heartbeat there,
made neither head nor tail of diagrams
in neuroscience, whose synapses can't conjure,
drawn instead by those twin Greek statues
on a cover, body in dialogue with mind.
The book opened in my hand to an avenue
of pebbles, riddles, thetas in the sand.

Wind on the spool to brother musician-poets
as one spoke stations like a list of ships,
again to sea-dark wine, a sound exhibit,
as the man now ghost heard the scratch of a nib
in the last November of the millennium,
to the Lamb in winter, where he was when you and I met,
to the April launch of *The Book of Love*
and the wake in the pub, as he took our hands like a priest.

Betterton Street

Maurice, see how these two are alike:
the small matter of a human brain
on an operating table and a bomb,
taken apart like a twelve-speed bike.

A tic of thought in the chamber creates speech.
In delivery a treaty is performed,
a poem fades, a mind becomes museum,
a fuse burns down to an iambic beat.

Always the fossil, not the quarry, lasts.
Communion's less bitter in water than in wine.
Shadows are doorways to a better time.
Everywhere peace breaks down like splintered glass.

Maybe It's Because

pavements are lined with the sense of
mother and other pedestrians even in
winter rain among tail-lights' flashing fins,
memories of being closer to the kerb,
an urge to climb up every step, then with
ten thousand men march back down again,
the intuition at two years old that you are
no one until you've jumped off the land's
rim into the Round Pond, the imperative
even now to follow the pebbledash path
through the park to Peter Pan, earth's
omphalos, your missing half, to catch fallen
leaves before they hit the ground, to be
spinning at the centre of a roundabout,
sliding down again and again and again,
adamantly refusing to leave the swings,
the adrenaline in the *Black Beauty* theme
before you could know what it means to
fall, to gallop headlong at an open field,
a mutual ambush of Cowboys and Indians,
the summer Eden of garden games of tag
with kids from the kibbutz of mansion flats.

The half-moon, iron bar I was lifted up
to touch, like a superstition, is still here
now by the Round Pond on Christmas Day
as I watch the angelica violet of the sunset,
seeing for the first time with adult eyes
what I have ever known, the daybreak of
dayclose disappearing into dusk, filling
the evening with echoes, laughter lapping
at the pond's shore, a lit path on the water
to remember all the seas that came after,
the familiar dereliction of the bandstand,
a statue to Physical Energy in bronze, cold
as death, yet spurring progress, tall avenues
of trees to everywhere and nowhere, white
innocence and wisdom of swans, clear as
the gardens now emptying, disclosing selves

unto themselves, undoing knots of memory,
unravelling the secret Acts of the Elfin Oak,
the four-sided fountain and shiny crow atop
roof and mast, flying steadily at the distance
on a course it sets itself and knows by heart.

In the Embankment Gardens I am centred
as Cleopatra's needle, stitching heaven,
as a tree needing earth, water, light,
seeing a heavy plane swim through the sky,
a solitary red balloon float on the current,
listening to the flock of noise, Big Ben,
a revving engine, a lit helicopter circling
to a mosquito dance, car horns conversing,
pleasantly invading space, unlike passing
families and each embracing brace skirting
over Sunday's surface silence, this frail
negotiated peace, the makeshift balance
at the turning of the week, the still calm
of the accounting firm's cathedral, while
trains are visibly entering and leaving
Charing Cross, knowing that I am here
and hearing my wristwatch pulse ring in
the soles and footsteps of another, startled
into pleasure by smacks of life, a birdcall,
a pigeon's flight, leaves buffeted by sound,
my blood pounding the heart's stable world.

New Year with Nelson
(1805-2005)

I'm seeing New Year in with Nelson.
You always know where you are with him.
Returning, he greets you
like a pub on a country lane.
He is a milestone, fixed through change,
through time, a sun dial, sun king.

He is above the screeching
of Saturday night revellers,
hanging out of limousines. Birds flock
to hear him mind reading.
He is a rock and we apostles.
He is the centre and squares the circle.

He is a pillar of reliability,
the tree you photographed in memory
from a childhood room, a dream
of stone to flesh and back again,
the fulcrum point of life and death,
a totem pole in the city's dance.

Ageless, he watches history,
every show of hands, each march.
He sees the wind-up cars, the trams,
the horse that came before the cart.
He is the bookend of Big Ben,
the cog round which an empire turned.

He's on display all week, all day,
another Atlas, a prince under glass,
a 24/7 mannequin, holding up a mirror
to light you to bed, to turn you to stone
and make you reflect on the core, the bone,
the eyes which saw before and are dead.

Under the Wave

It's the moment in the Japanese print
when the tsunami freezes, the instant
when the known giant of Mt Fuji shrinks
to one more breaker in the distance,

before high cold smashes the life in each boat,
a patient's graph before a monitor blips,
the note in the score where hearts miss a beat,
the King Kong screen before the first plane hits,

a Mercedes before its Hades descent,
an Omagh second before grief erupts,
the space before New Year strikes with Big Ben,
the deaths before fireworks blast and gates shut.

Good Friday

Rise early and head for the City,
following the paperchase of names,
letting words tell the way,
navigating by a plot you choose
from Apothecary's Street
to the sanctuary of St Dunstan-in-the-East.

There will be no commuters today,
though you may meet with an agency nurse
who will ask you the way to Barts,
or road sweepers pushing carts like prams
and bearing the crossed wood of brooms,
and a man sleeping rough to whom you will give.

Later, night buses will circulate like blood,
keeping the lungs of London moving.
And though this is not the Blitz,
beacons will pulse morse code,
while some will set out on the road to darkness
and return with Antigone, or Christ, at new dawn.

May Sunday

And do they see the stucco peeling?
BETJEMAN

As we circumvent the Gothic plot,
locked silence of museum stone,
Victorian doors from street to past,
single file echoes, turban of the Onion's dome,

tin hat brass of industry and empire,
high arched windows of church, or state,
the fortress yields to library ivy, a corridor
to the marble of draughtsboard distance

and suddenly all the town's stucco peels
to the memory of an overheard rally,
Scargill's voice, live from a cream marquee
in the Imperial Gardens in the Eighties.

On Byron Ward

I am diffusing a cigarette
before it detonates someone's heart.
At the handover of death and birth
relativity is the letter U reversed.

Landing precedes take-off,
just as *Go!* slows to *Stop!*
The pyramid of human needs
starts with, not climbs to, creativity.

Summer branches nod 'A-men'
to one from a line of clergymen.
You know you're in the loony bin
when you answer aloud your own question.

I was taught to sign my name, 'Sarah',
but I could choose to write it 'S Eire'.
I'm not dangerous to know, have no insanity,
am neither mad, nor bad, but this Act makes me angry.

Looking Back

There are some who crack every spring, every pretty ring time. It must be borne on the mad March air. One morning you're minding other people's business, the next seeing death everywhere. Take a fear, any fear, and times by the power of the IRA over Al-Qaida, and next thing you'll know you're knocking down dustbins in the Strand, running from police vans, wanting civil servants to evacuate ministries, asking a stranger if you can drop a Clanger by the Cenotaph, a pink knitted Clanger. And it was the death of the Pope, not the author, the General Election, men in combats, the washing, the washing, the red and the black, the soldier statues and the street signs, street signs, every one leading to logic, peculiar logic, the crossed thetas, dotted iotas, the meaning and shape of letters down ages, the worlds turned upside down, the sand which has run and is yet to run, the promise of sacred hearts to come, the sequence of names, patterns of initials, the waste of lives on battlefields, the trials of lives in hospitals, the ignorance of blind trust, the cruelty of those who put to the test, the folly of those who question not, the influence of sights and sounds, the conditioned repetitions, descending notes with dates in ascension, the good and the bad of names, pedestrians, crowds, points of the compass, clocked-up hours, the walkabouts by day and night to map, guard, keep watch, alive, to lift, to birth, to swear to try.

Messenger

No one listens to the old man
or earth, the matriarch, as she spins
her web from Bear to Orion,
to Tiresias, although he sees
through the eye of every coming storm,
to the pupil's song on ebony keys,
or history's footfalls, as she leaves
the door ajar for her return.
Lady Macbeth will never believe
Cassandra's commentary in the margin,
just as we too can't conceive
a living room, pregnant with grief,
as a clock ticks and a body is cooling
like a star, or pan of milk on a ring.